THE
FUTURE OF GREEK STUDIES

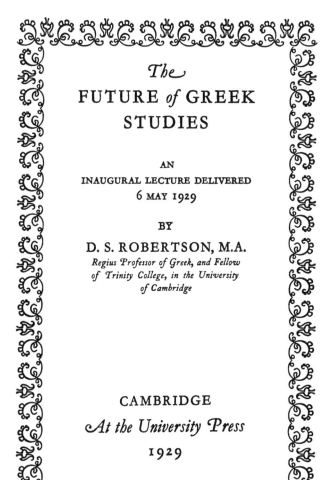

The
FUTURE *of* GREEK STUDIES

AN
INAUGURAL LECTURE DELIVERED
6 MAY 1929

BY

D. S. ROBERTSON, M.A.
Regius Professor of Greek, and Fellow
of Trinity College, in the University
of Cambridge

CAMBRIDGE
At the University Press
1929

CAMBRIDGE
UNIVERSITY PRESS

University Printing House, Cambridge CB2 8BS, United Kingdom

Published in the United States of America by Cambridge University Press, New York

Cambridge University Press is part of the University of Cambridge.

It furthers the University's mission by disseminating knowledge in the pursuit of education, learning and research at the highest international levels of excellence.

www.cambridge.org
Information on this title: www.cambridge.org/9781107666535

© Cambridge University Press 1929

First published 1929
Re-issued 2014

A catalogue record for this publication is available from the British Library

ISBN 978-1-107-66653-5 Paperback

The
FUTURE OF GREEK STUDIES

THE tradition of the Regius Professorship
of Greek in this University stretches back
almost to the dawn of Greek studies in
England, for Sir John Cheke, its first holder,
who "taught Cambridge and King Edward
Greek," was born when Erasmus was lecturing
in Queens'.

A Chair so ancient, made illustrious by
such scholars as Porson and Dobree, is no
easy heritage. A newly elected Professor may
be expected in his Inaugural Lecture to state
his opinion of the proper functions of his
Chair, and to indicate the lines on which he
hopes to develop them; and where the Chair
is a new or recent creation he may feel himself a pioneer, whose task is to mark out a new
path in University studies: but a Greek Professor, especially if he brings, as I do, little

enough of solid performance in scholarship, must feel it to be his first duty to understand the aims and methods of his predecessors, his first hope not to fall too far short of their achievement.

It is with such feelings that I wish, before saying anything of my own views, to speak briefly of the three scholars who within the limits of my own memory have adorned this Chair, without omitting some of their illustrious contemporaries, no longer living, to whom Fate was not kind.

When I came into residence twenty-five years ago Sir Richard Jebb had already held the Professorship for fifteen years and the greater part of his classical work was done, though his Bacchylides did not appear till 1905. He died in the same year, and to my deep regret I scarcely knew him personally, though I attended with profit two courses of his lectures. Jebb's great achievement in scholarship is a matter of history, which stands in no need of eulogy. It is true that in linguistic analysis, in textual criticism, and in literary interpretation later scholars have found much to question, and it is perhaps commoner to-day to hear his work quoted for blame than for praise. But such criticism assumes, or at least ought to assume, that the general distinction and excellence of his work are above question, and, even had he done nothing else, the seven volumes of his Sophocles would remain a solid and splendid monument of learning and judgment, almost unique in modern English scholarship.

In the closing years of Jebb's tenure the prospects of Greek in Cambridge were singularly bright. At the opening of the twentieth century the University was rich in scholars clearly worthy to hold the Regius Professorship. One of the most brilliant, indeed, Robert Alexander Neil, died prematurely in the first year of the century, leaving little tangible record of his vast and humane learning and exquisite scholarship, except his posthumous edition of the *Knights* of Aristophanes. But, despite this great loss, when Jebb himself died four years later, the five candidates who came forward, all residents, were of extraordinary distinction. The cumulative effect of

7

the five Praelections which in obedience to the old Statutes they delivered in the Senate House can never be forgotten by anyone who listened to them, and can still be felt by those who study the volume in which they were afterwards published. The following years, however, were disastrous, and though the Electors' choice had fallen on the oldest of the five, Henry Jackson, he long outlived all the rest, except one, William Ridgeway. Three of the younger men, Verrall, Adam, and Headlam, died prematurely within ten years of Jebb.

Of these three I owe personally far the most to Verrall, who was my Director of Studies for the whole of my undergraduate time. When I first saw him he was already crippled by the disease which killed him, but with amazing courage he still showed himself the most enthralling of lecturers and the most sympathetic of personal teachers. He was a man who inspired in all who knew him a feeling of intense personal devotion of which I cannot bring myself to say more in a public lecture.

Of his published work it is needless to speak to a Cambridge audience. The unsleeping alertness of his mind, the freshness of his observation, the sparkling brilliance of his wit make his books and essays a perpetual joy to read. It cannot, of course, be denied that he was often perverse and fanciful, and that sometimes, as in his treatment of the plot of the *Agamemnon*, he seems to most scholars to have shot very wide of the mark. But his criticism, whether right or wrong, was always stimulating and challenging, and his work on Euripides, whatever its faults of detail, made an epoch in the sympathetic appreciation of fifth-century Greek thought. It is probably difficult for those who knew his books but never heard his lectures or his conversation to believe the truth that his writing, fascinating as it is, is only a pale shadow of his spoken word. The influence of his books and lectures in awakening the minds of generations of students to a new appreciation of Greek poetry can hardly be over-estimated, though this influence, as Headlam felt, had dangerous elements. But on the balance it was infinitely more helpful than harmful, and it has left an ineffaceable mark on English scholarship.

From James Adam I had some personal kindness, but I knew him chiefly from his books, and, though I have studied those with keen interest, I do not approach them as an expert, and my admiration of them can only be an echo of the general verdict of more competent critics. In my first year I heard his admirable lectures on Later Greek Philosophy, and I was amazed, as all his hearers must have been, at his power of interesting a very large undergraduate audience in the details even of those schools of thought for which he himself had obviously little admiration. The secret lay, I think, chiefly in that burning enthusiasm for Plato which could always be felt as the background and atmosphere of all that he said and wrote.

The last of these three, Walter Headlam, was by general consent the first Grecian of his generation, a man obviously marked out to enrich the traditions of the Greek Chair. I did not know him as his King's pupils knew him, but I had the delight of meeting him once or twice, and I heard the famous lectures on Greek Lyric Metre, of which the substance was afterwards published in the *Journal of Hellenic Studies*. I shall return to Headlam's work at a later point: for the moment I will only remark that he had conceived the proper approach to the study of classical Greek poetry in so nobly comprehensive a spirit that when he died suddenly in 1908 he had not given the world more than a foretaste of the work which he would certainly have accomplished had he lived. He was still mobilizing in distant theatres many of the forces which would ultimately have converged, with incalculable effect, on his central study of the poetry of Aeschylus. His true greatness has never been fully appreciated outside England.

Henry Jackson, who held the Chair from 1906 till 1921, was far better known to me than either Adam or Headlam, and I owe him many personal debts of which I will not attempt to speak. He has left no written memorial that could make intelligible to a later generation the intellectual and moral influence which he exerted for half a century in his College and in the University. That influence is no riddle to those who knew him, for his personality was irresistible. To him the Greek Chair came very late in life, when his best original work was already done, and when he had long been firmly settled in admirable habits of lecturing and class instruction. His appointment by his College as Praelector in Ancient Philosophy had already freed him from the ordinary routine of individual College teaching in Composition and Translation, so that his election to the Professorship made little difference to his activities. He continued to lecture only on philosophical subjects, but all those who knew him were aware of the depth and range of his scholarship: the suggestion, sometimes made, that he lacked interest in other branches of Greek literature was entirely false. Of his original work in Greek philosophy, as of James Adam's, I am not myself competent to speak, but I learnt from the personal experience of his elementary lectures and from the talk of his more advanced pupils something of his genius for teaching and of his extraordinary power of holding and inspiring his listeners. No one who knew him could help feeling the width and certainty of his knowledge of Greek language and thought. The accident that I was Secretary of the Classical Board for the years just before his death brought me into frequent contact with him at a time when ill-health was cutting him off from much social intercourse, and I know that, in spite of a fitfully failing memory, the freshness and vigour of his classical interests continued undimmed to the very end of his life.

When Jackson died in 1921, William Ridgeway was the only candidate surviving from 1905, and he was again unsuccessful. Of Ridgeway, as of Verrall, I find it difficult to speak in a public lecture, and I will not attempt any personal appreciation. Everyone who knew him, even slightly, must have felt the presence of one of the most extraordinary and masterful personalities that Cambridge can ever have held: his friends knew also how generous, loyal, and lovable was his character, and no death in my recollection has left a more irreplaceable gap. His classical scholarship had obvious faults which sprang, I think, chiefly from his weakness in strict logic: but it had also unique merits, for it was an organic part of an unexampled acquaintance, marvellous in its range and depth, with the cultures, past and present, of the whole human race. His mind surveyed a world of phenomena, and forced them into a vast framework of original classification. Some of that classification was arbitrary and premature, and in detail much of his work is already obsolete: but the width of his knowledge enabled him to set countless facts for the first time in true perspective, and for sheer grandeur of conception his best work still stands unapproached. Yet the mental power which could be felt in his speech was not fully expressed in his writings, and with him, as with Jackson, the intense admiration of his pupils will perhaps never be wholly intelligible to those who did not see and know him.

Of the other unsuccessful candidates of 1921 I will mention only one, the greatest and most brilliant scholar, Arthur Platt, and of him I will not try to speak: not because I knew him too well, for I barely met him, but because what is to be said of him has already found perfect expression.

I come last, before passing to more general topics, to my immediate predecessor, Dr Pearson, who was elected in 1921 and resigned, after seven years' tenure, in 1928. The same accident which kept me in touch with Jackson just before his death, my Secretaryship of the Classical Board, brought me into close contact with Dr Pearson immediately after his return to Cambridge, and I do not find it easy to remember that my acquaintance with him dates back no further. Of all the candidates of 1921 Dr Pearson could show the greatest body of solid research brilliantly achieved. Even had no account been taken of his work on later Greek philosophy, for instance, or of his preparation for the press of Headlam's still chaotic notes on the *Agamemnon* of Aeschylus, the three volumes of

Fragments, with which he completed Jebb's Sophocles, volumes which form one of the greatest works of modern scholarship, gave him an overwhelming claim to Jackson's succession.

If it is hard to speak of some of those scholars, no longer living, whom I have known and loved, it is much harder to speak of Dr Pearson, who is still happily among us, and still pursuing his admirable work on Sophocles, of whom he published, while holding the Professorship, the best existing text. The debt which Greek scholarship in this University owes to his masterly example and sympathetic helpfulness is known to all who have followed the history of Cambridge Classics during the last seven years. To follow him is difficult indeed.

I am tempted to dwell at greater length on the work of earlier Professors, and to trace back the history of the Greek Chair to the heroic age of Porson, and beyond, though in some moods the thought of my predecessors' distinction is almost as much overwhelming as stimulating. But for such a task I am not adequately equipped, and it would in any case take me too far afield. However shy I may feel of talking about the more general aspects of the study of Greek, it is a duty laid on me by this office, and I cannot shirk it.

Yet I should be lacking in piety if I turned from past to present without honouring the name of the Royal Founder of this Chair, King Henry the Eighth, Founder also of my College, and part-Founder of my School, Westminster, a School which can now claim nine of the thirty-three holders of this Professorship.

In one of the last conversations that I had with Henry Jackson he said to me, with a curious detachment from which all personal feeling seemed to be eliminated, "It is strange that I should have lived to see the end of Greek studies in Cambridge." I do not think that he said this from a feeling that there was a lack of scholars worthy to carry on the traditions of his Chair, but because it seemed to him that the supply of undergraduate students was shrinking so fast that it was doomed in the near future to virtual extinction. His belief was exaggerated on the evidence available at the moment, and in the last seven or eight years the current all over the country has set in the opposite direction, and the Cambridge Classical School, so far as the number of students is a test, is now in a very flourishing state. The causes that govern such fluctuations are extremely difficult to analyze, and, though there seems now good ground for optimism, it is obvious that Greek is a branch of study which depends for its prosperity on a belief in its intrinsic value and interest scarcely susceptible of definite proof. It can still, perhaps, count on the continuance of a rather indefinite traditional prestige, but it cannot, like some branches of Natural Science, hope for any large measure of incidental support from those who care only for what they believe to promote the direct material benefit of the human race.

It is therefore inevitable that students and teachers of Greek should ask themselves at least as often as those of other subjects, what is the real purpose of their life-work, and how far they can justify its claims.

The problem is, of course, twofold: first, why Greek should be studied by students not intending to be specialists, and secondly why it should be studied by specialists. The relative importance attached to the two halves of the problem will differ according to temperaments. No one much acquainted with classical scholars can be unaware that some care chiefly for the advance of their subject in itself and for its own sake and do not in truth very much mind how many men and women equip themselves for life by a general classical training: while what others have really at heart is precisely the provision of a general classical training for as large a number of students as possible. But most scholars feel the importance of both aspects.

It must be admitted that it is difficult for a classical scholar who cares chiefly for the advance of his subject to approach the question of its value as a general training quite impartially. I remember a non-classical undergraduate delighting Verrall by the remark that he had always supposed that the only purpose of the Classics as a School and University subject was to keep up the supply of teachers to train other teachers, but that from talking to a fellow-undergraduate (who was in fact Kenneth Freeman) he had begun to wonder if perhaps there might not be something more in it after all.

Every scholar interested in the future of his subject must inevitably desire that the ranks of scholarship should be steadily recruited, and it is obvious that this can only happen on two conditions: first, that there should be a supply of young men at the end of their undergraduate time, qualified by training and enthusiasm for undertaking such work: and, secondly, that there should be teaching posts available offering them the hope of a permanent career. There is doubtless a danger of unconscious bias from such considerations, but this danger is not peculiar to Classics: and if Classics were once a vested interest in a position of peculiarly artificial strength, they certainly are so no more.

What then are the grounds on which those who believe in the value of general classical training, and especially in the value of Greek, can support their claims? I am conscious here, as in many other parts of this lecture, that I am going over familiar ground, and that I am in danger of repeating what has been dinned into people's ears till they are sick of listening: but champions of the Classics have not been vocal in Cambridge since the last Compulsory Greek controversy, nearly a quarter of a century ago, and I shall dwell chiefly on those aspects of the matter which especially appeal to my own temperament.

The value of the Greek language, taken by itself, as a mental training is perhaps sometimes exaggerated, though I feel little doubt that it helps, more than most foreign languages, towards precision and subtlety of thought and expression. At the same time the necessity of mastering the language, as the indispensable foundation of all further advance, cannot be over-emphasized. It is idle to pretend that Greek is a language that allows of short cuts or rapid acquisition by simple reading on the basis of a smattering of grammar. In the learning of Greek, as my predecessor, I have heard, was fond of telling his pupils at Dulwich, the gods have put sweat on the path of achievement. Indeed this irremovable difficulty of the actual language has always seemed to me the chief danger to the future of Greek as an instrument of general training. It is perhaps a little too difficult, and there is some truth in the complaint that, for many of those who do not carry it beyond the school stage, Greek is dropped just before the ridge is mounted from which wide views of its delightful landscape begin to open out.

This problem, however, concerns University teachers only indirectly, for in my experience very few of those who study Greek as undergraduates here feel at the end of their time that they are sent away empty. The Universities still receive, and seem likely to receive, a steady supply of students adequately grounded in Greek, and ready and eager to get what good they can out of the Classics: the problem for the University teacher is what that good really is, and how it can be given.

At the Universities, of course, as at the

Schools, the fundamental thing is still the learning of the language, an activity that all serious scholars must continue unremittingly to the end of their lives. In effect, for undergraduate students, this means chiefly continuous personal teaching in the Colleges, an indispensable means of testing and sharpening their knowledge of usage and their feeling for idiom and style. But it is easier at the Universities than at the Schools to feel clearly that the study of language is ultimately a means to an end. That end, so far as the majority of students is concerned, is perfectly clear and unambiguous: Greek is learnt for the sake of reading and appreciating the works of the greatest Greek writers, including the philosophers. That is to my mind almost the whole justification for the general teaching of the subject, and it is overwhelmingly sufficient. Knowledge of the language is of course not the only necessary condition for appreciation of the literature, though it is far the most important: nor should appreciation of the literature be interpreted too narrowly, as if it were confined to the strictly aesthetic valuation of the poems, plays, and prose-writings.

Those merits are, indeed, so transcendent that this alone would be more than enough. It is difficult to speak in this matter without the appearance of exaggeration, and without risking the censure of those who prefer to enjoy Greek literature in silence, without proclaiming its merits to the world. That is, I think, the instinctive reaction of most scholars and it is certainly mine. But I know from experience that such reticence is often misunderstood, and I feel that, in arguing the claims of a classical training, I should be hiding the truth, if I did not give some expression to my own sense of the unique and unapproachable excellence of Greek poetry and prose, and to my conviction that no later European literature, however splendid, can replace the Greek as a foundation of culture, a standard of taste, and a source of imperishable wonder and delight.

But, apart from the absolute merits of their greatest achievements, direct acquaintance with the literature of Greece and Rome (for the two must be studied together) makes living to modern men, as nothing else can, the social and political conditions, and the general and philosophic thought of the civilization on which our own is chiefly based: it shows us the ideas that govern a great part of our taste and conduct, as they grew and spread before their branches were entangled with the different beliefs and standards that entered Europe in the first centuries of the Roman Empire. The value to men of every variety of belief and temperament of this direct contact with the pre-Christian Western world seems to me quite inestimably great.

I would not seem to underestimate the importance, to the ordinary student, of real comprehension of the political history, the archaeology, or the philology of Greece and Rome: some knowledge of history in particular is absolutely essential, and the more the student can learn of all these matters the better. But the field is vast, and for most students the time is short: and nothing can compensate for failure to read and assimilate the great works of ancient literature, as masterpieces of incomparably subtle and intellectual art, and as conscious or unconscious mirrors of racial and individual reactions to the problems of existence.

At the same time it is extremely important that the classical curriculum here should be so designed as to enable men who wish to concentrate on any particular branch of more specialized study to make a start and to begin to understand the nature of the problems and of the evidence in the particular field that may interest them. With all its defects, which most classical teachers here would admit, I think that on the whole the present Classical Tripos, with its Second Part divided between general and specialized study, does fairly well meet the necessities of the situation.

I am conscious that in laying so much stress on the literary side of general classical training I am courting the comment that the power of original literary criticism is a rare and special gift, to which the classical teacher, except by an unusual coincidence, cannot and should not lay claim. I admit that this is true, and that the classical teacher's first and chief duty is simply to enable his pupils to understand the meaning of the books which they read. But though literary appreciation must doubtless be left in the main to the students' own taste, it does not seem to me either possible or desirable for the teacher to draw a rigid line between explanation and literary criticism, or to suppress his own preferences and such grounds for those preferences as he feels able to formulate. It is true that the thing can only too easily be overdone, and that students are justly sensitive to aesthetic dictation. I do not forget my feelings when I accidentally saw a pupil's notes on one of my own lectures, in which I fancied that I had analyzed with some felicity the artistic qualities of a series of Pindar's Odes: my comments were summarized in one sentence, followed by three exclamation marks, "This Ode *also* is Pindar's finest."

I now come to the other main aspect of classical work at the Universities, the advancement of learning. For any Professor this is at least as important as the question of teaching: indeed the Statutory definition of his

duties mentions research before instruction—
"It shall be the duty of a Professor both to devote himself to research and the advancement of knowledge in his subject and to give instruction to students." Historically, I suppose, the Greek Chair was founded in order that there might always be in the University one person qualified to teach the Greek language: and it was doubtless because men came to the University with a knowledge of Latin, and because there was in any case no danger of any lack of qualified teachers, that Henry the Eighth did not think it necessary to create also a Chair of Latin. The Greek Professor is happily no longer expected to teach students their alphabet or declensions: but I think that any holder of the Chair must feel that his first duty is still to know the Greek language. Knowledge of Greek is still the fundamental condition of all his activity, and undue ignorance of it the least excusable of all imaginable defects. I say "undue ignorance," for even approximately complete knowledge is an unattainable ideal: but any Greek Professor must feel that on him more

than on anyone else it is incumbent never to relax the attempt to enlarge and purify his mastery of this subtle, fascinating, and incomparable speech.

Such study of the Greek language may be not merely the fundamental condition of a Greek scholar's work, but, if his chief interest happen to lie in grammatical analysis or in the exact study of verbal usage, it may in fact be his work: and in spite of the labours of generations of scholars there still remain wide fields that call for an indefinite amount of intensive study, fields in which work can be done of permanent and indisputable value. But to most scholars the problems presented by the written and material remains of Greek antiquity appeal from so many sides that purely linguistic investigations do not satisfy their ambitions. To me personally the supreme attraction of Greece as a field of study lies first in the extraordinary interest of every manifestation of the spiritual activity of the Greeks. The quality of their best work, whether in poetry or philosophy, in sculpture, painting, or architecture, is so undeniably excellent, so infinitely rich and subtle, that the student's worst doubts in his blackest moods of depression can never touch the intrinsic value of the thing studied, even if he be concerned with some of the less immediately interesting parts of the field, but only the value of his own work. The attraction lies secondly in the extreme complexity of the material available, and in the fact that its superficially most diverse manifestations are so closely interwoven that the mind which attempts to deepen its understanding of any one aspect must never cease to strive, however inadequately, to conceive this aspect as a part of a much greater whole.

It would perhaps be difficult for most scholars settled in one branch of original research to say exactly what led them to concentrate on that particular subject. In some cases, no doubt, the answer would be that the choice was originally dictated by the necessity of finding, at the end of their undergraduate careers, a subject of enquiry offering good hope of tangible results from one or two years' work. No one who has been consulted by classical students at this stage of their lives is likely to underrate the difficulty of suggesting suitable subjects: indeed this difficulty is one of the disadvantages of Classics in comparison with some other branches of University study. It is not surprising that subjects so chosen sometimes fail to reflect the student's instinctive inclinations and do not always set him on a path which he is likely to follow in later life in the intervals of his teaching work. But I do not wish to exaggerate the frequency of such false starts, and I think that in any case they usually do less harm than might be feared. A certain proportion of students, in Classics as in every other branch of study, of course find during their first years of original work that they have in truth no instinctive impulse towards research, and such men, if they follow an academic career, will naturally concentrate in later life on teaching or on administration. But those who have the instinct of research, even if their first choice does not prove permanently satisfying, will probably discover incidentally, from some side-issue of their investigations, where their interest and competence in fact chiefly lie: and they will have received a training in method and a perception of the nature of evidence that will serve them thenceforth in whatever department they ultimately enter with a really free and conscious choice.

Students of other subjects sometimes say or hint that as a field of research the writings of the Greek and Latin authors are in truth worked out: or they will at most admit that modern excavation has provided in addition to much purely archaeological material, the importance of which no one can deny, a limited number of literary inscriptions and papyrus fragments on which some genuinely original work can be done. The value of such new material is, of course, enormous, not only for its intrinsic interest, but also because it so often enlarges and completes existing knowledge or proves the necessity of a reconsideration of received beliefs: it is obvious that in no other direction is there so good a chance of startling discovery. Yet the suggestion that this is the only or even the chief direction in which knowledge can be advanced rests on a complete misapprehension. What is, I think, true is that really valuable research in most classical fields is now very difficult, and calls for high qualities of mind. We are no longer, like the scholars of the fifteenth and sixteenth centuries, faced with great masses of unexplored Greek and Latin literature, newly recovered from the obscurity of monastic libraries and only beginning to be widely accessible to trained students. The pioneer work is largely done, and the student who starts research to-day is apt at the outset to be overwhelmed by the mass of modern literature concerning his special subject, which must, he feels, have exhausted all that there is to say. But this feeling rarely survives a penetrating first-hand acquaintance with any particular branch of study. The deeper he delves, the clearer does it usually become that of the long series of workers whose accumulated prestige terrified him at the start only a few have brought to their task a sufficient equipment of knowledge or intelligence to make their work altogether satisfactory.

Few, perhaps, will have failed to contribute something to the advancement of knowledge, but he will often find surprisingly little steady progress and sure consolidation of gains. The really great names are few and far between, and he may find that the best work on his subject was done in any century from the fifteenth to the twentieth, and that the idleness or imprudence of later scholars has consigned to oblivion truths that were seized by Beroaldus, Scaliger, or Bentley.

I think that it would be unfair to infer from this uncertainty of progress, so alien, I imagine, to the experience of mathematicians or natural scientists, that classical scholarship has lacked, in comparison with other subjects, its full share of able and industrious men. I think, on the contrary, that it is an historical fact that until recent times an exceptionally high proportion of the best intellect of all European countries has been turned in this direction. The reason lies rather in the extremely difficult nature of the material, and in the fact that the truth or falsehood of many of the conclusions of classical scholarship is not susceptible of a plain mathematical demonstration. The conclusions rest rather on a subtle balance of probabilities, which must be weighed by a judgment naturally sensitive to niceties of thought and speech and capable of a sustained and unrelaxed grasp of a very wide range of knowledge. To appreciate the justice or to perceive the error of Bentley's or Porson's judgment on a difficult point of language does not, of course, require qualities of mind equal to Bentley's or Porson's, but it does call for comparable qualities, and such qualities are inevitably rare.

I do not, however, wish to exaggerate the unprogressive nature of classical scholarship. Many of the discoveries and generalizations of the greatest scholars of every generation have established themselves beyond all cavil or dispute, and have become part of the common store of learning: and in so far as the advance of knowledge consists in the accumulation and sifting of definite and verifiable facts, there has been since the fifteenth century a steady improvement in the equipment available to the classical scholar.

Manuscripts have been collated, fragments of lost writers collected, chronology established, linguistic phenomena investigated and classified, the rhythms of poetry and prose studied and tabulated, concordances compiled, and a hundred other invaluable services performed. The modern student starts with enormous advantages, for which he ought to be unspeakably grateful to the unselfish labours of countless predecessors and contemporaries: it is difficult not to take these advantages for granted, or to realize how stupendous, in their absence, was the achievement of such a scholar as Scaliger. Yet despite the accumulation of such material, and despite the help that it has given modern scholars, how few are the authors and how few the problems on which we can feel that anything approaching the last word has been said! The last word can of course never be said, in this or in any other department of literary or historical enquiry. The nature of the material studied makes finality unthinkable, for the expression in written speech of the thought and feelings of men may be considered from so many angles and is rooted in so much that eludes confident analysis that, even when earlier students have brought the widest knowledge and the keenest intellect to their task, new problems will always present themselves to the minds of a later generation. And this is true to a peculiar degree of the material which confronts the classical student. He has to interpret the infinitesimally scanty wreckage that has survived by the slenderest threads from a vast world of ceaseless mental activity. If we think only of Greek literary works, how tiny a proportion even of what reached the scholars of Alexandria has survived to our own day! We may take as an example one branch of literature, which happens to interest me to an exceptional degree, Greek comedy: it flourished for centuries: we know the names of nearly 200 poets, and we have the titles of about 1600 plays. Yet, apart from ancient quotations, Latin adaptations and the wrecks of a few plays recovered in papyri, we possess only 11 Greek comedies, all composed by a single poet within a period of forty years. There lies therefore behind the

37

writings which we struggle to reconstruct and interpret so vast a background of darkness and obscurity that in our wider and bolder conclusions there must always remain an element of reserve and uncertainty.

I have perhaps spent too long in generalizations, without speaking in detail of the sort of work in which I conceive the future of classical scholarship chiefly to lie. It is, of course, difficult for any student to speak otherwise than in wide and loose language of other aspects of scholarship than those which his own circumstances or inclinations have led him to study with close attention. He is conscious, when he gets outside his own particular subject, that he is uncertain of his ground, and that there must be among his listeners many far better qualified than himself to deal with the matters on which he touches, many who will feel that he is fumbling at locks whose working he does not really understand. I shall therefore not attempt to speak of such important and fruitful fields of research as Greek history and philosophy; indeed I shall say little except about one particular subject on which my own attention, through many years of scattered activity, has gradually been concentrating.

Yet there is one important branch of classical study, also largely outside my range, about which I would first speak very briefly, for the reason that I am, I think, more closely in touch with it than were any of my predecessors in this Chair, namely archaeology. I studied archaeology in the old Second Part of the Classical Tripos, and, though my general knowledge of the subject has never been deep, the preparation necessary for the lectures on Greek and Roman architecture which I have delivered since 1911, and for some written work which has been their outcome, has kept me for twenty years in some sort of contact with archaeological literature and with students and teachers of archaeology.

The proper position of this subject in the general scheme of classical teaching has always seemed to me a very difficult question. The literary field is so vast that I do not think that any substantial archaeological element can fairly be introduced into the earlier stages of classical training at Cambridge: it is essentially a subject for the Second Part of the Tripos. I think that the most that can be done for students for the First Part of the Tripos is to give them the chance of getting a glimpse of the material monuments in relation both to political history and to the development of art. Something is already done in this direction, but there is perhaps room for more.

The instinct for artistic form is somewhat rare and it has little necessary connexion with the qualities that make for excellence in literary scholarship: but it is very desirable that those who may possess this instinct should be awakened early to its unique and irreplaceable value for the study of ancient life. That value is not always understood or admitted. The importance of some kinds of material evidence, such as inscriptions and coins, especially for political and religious history, is of course too obvious for anyone to deny, but I think that in general there is still in this matter a good deal of misappre-

hension by pure scholars, who tend to mini-
mize the importance for the understanding
of the ancient mind of the study of material
remains, except in so far as they illustrate
definite historical problems or particular pas-
sages of literary works. This attitude seems
to me quite mistaken. Everyone will, of
course, agree that buildings, statues, vases,
and coins (if they are to be studied at all)
must be studied for their own sakes and on
their own lines of development, and that
their history must be pursued forwards and
backwards, whether or not they can be
brought at any given point into relation with
literary evidence. Archaeological discoveries
which throw fresh light on literature or history are equally delightful to students in both
fields, and it would be stupid and ungrateful
to underrate their importance: but the remains of ancient art have a far wider and
deeper appeal to all those whose interest lies
ultimately in the quality and temper of the
Greek and Roman mind. Such pages, for
instance, as those which Professor Beazley of
Oxford has given to archaic, fifth-century, and

fourth-century art in the *Cambridge Ancient History* exquisitely illuminate and interpret some of the subtlest of the Greeks' spiritual creations. Such evidence as that which he uses is complementary to that of literature: it often confirms and reinforces it, but often it is fullest for places and periods where literary evidence is scanty or absent. Its full appreciation calls for special aptitude and for some special training, but its value will be ignored only by those who are not competent to appraise it. Of the delightful things of Hellas, in Pindar's words, we have received no scanty gift: none surpass in permanent value the architecture, sculpture, and vase-painting of the sixth and fifth centuries, and the gods' glorious gifts are not lightly to be cast aside.

But of archaeology I have said enough for my purpose, perhaps too much. I think that I can judge and appreciate research in that field, but I am well aware that I am not qualified to further it, and I must turn to matters in which, rightly or wrongly, I feel myself to be more competent.

I have already remarked that I will not

try to speak of strictly philosophical or historical research, for they also lie outside my range, and I will confine myself henceforth to the subject of Greek literature. Here there seem to me to be two or three chief distinguishable lines on which research naturally moves. A scholar may choose to fix his attention chiefly on some particular phenomenon of language, style, or substance, and to follow this thread through authors of a selected class or of a selected period or even through the whole range of Greek literature. Again, he may choose to concentrate his interest on some comparatively neglected author —and of such there is still no lack—and to produce an intensive study of the textual, linguistic, and substantial problems which his works present. Or lastly he may be ambitious enough to attempt a fresh attack on the works of one of the unchallenged masters of prose or poetry, who have exerted the minds of the finest scholars of every generation. All three methods can be illustrated from the life of Walter Headlam. He had always in mind the criticism and interpreta-

tion of Aeschylus, who irresistibly attracted
him as one of the greatest poets and one of
the noblest spirits of all time, and he was
always working at his plays, and especially
at the *Agamemnon*. At the same time he
initiated, before his premature death, a new
and valuable approach to the problems presented by lyric metre through the whole
range of ancient verse: and he also threw
himself into the task of establishing and eluci-
dating the newly discovered text of the Mimes
of Herodas.

It is no accident that Headlam worked on
all these lines and more: for, though a scholar
may well prefer to leave the very greatest
authors untouched, except incidentally, if he
does touch them, he cannot but feel that at
the present day the best hope of advance lies
in the widest possible plan of attack, and in
the intensive study of many other authors
and of many special problems which affect
a wider field. It was in this spirit that A. W.
Mair, by whose tragic death Greek scholarship has lately suffered irreparable loss, gave
years of his life to the study of such feeble

verse-writers as Lycophron and Oppian, in order to fit himself to interpret one of the greatest and most difficult of all poets, Aeschylus' contemporary, Pindar.

My own chief interest happens to agree with Mair's. I have read and lectured on Pindar for years, but I find it difficult to express in words at once how fascinating and how remote seems to me the goal at which a serious student of Pindar is bound to aim. The problems that face such a student are almost overwhelming in their complexity and difficulty. What does not the man who would really understand Pindar need to understand? The social and political atmosphere and development not only of his birthplace Thebes, but also of the many Greek cities for whose kings and citizens he wrote: the origin and significance of Greek athletic festivals: the epic and lyric poetry on which he was bred, and the musical and poetical traditions which he inherited: the artistic and literary movements which he witnessed and promoted: the ancient moral and political conceptions which he expounded and modified: the religious

45

beliefs and movements among which he worked.

These are only a few of the general problems which form a background to the interpretation of Pindar's work. Apart from such wide considerations, it is the first duty of the student of his poems to face in detail countless difficult questions of metre, dialect, and expression: he must make his own careful examination of the tradition of the text, and of the relics of ancient learning embedded in the scholiasts' tangled commentaries. He must try to understand for themselves and to correlate with Pindar's surviving writings the many fragments, often mutilated and corrupt, which are quoted by later Greek writers, and the broken mass of fresh material which the labours of excavators and papyrologists are still recovering from Egypt: he must study the methods and opinions of the ancient critics, and he must endeavour to trace Pindar's influence on later literature and to wring, if possible, from his readers and imitators some fresh light on the lost originals which they knew.

Such a scheme is, of course, too vast for one man to hope to execute. Some of the problems at which I have hinted are perhaps insoluble: there are others, such as those of Greek music, which may some day yield their secrets to experts but cannot profitably be touched by an ordinary scholar. My own strongest wish is to advance the knowledge of Pindar, but my purpose in saying what I have said is to indicate at once the attraction and difficulties of such a task, rather than to suggest that I can hope to go far towards its accomplishment. Yet those who remember Headlam may well wish to work with some such ideal, however remote, in their minds, and to aim at combining intense concentration on one great writer with the widest possible general study of the vast and magnificent field of the literature, history, and archaeology of Greece: a field of inexhaustible interest, whose incomparable splendour, through all fluctuations of fashion and taste, can never cease to fascinate and enthral the minds of men.

www.ingramcontent.com/pod-product-compliance
Ingram Content Group UK Ltd.
Pitfield, Milton Keynes, MK11 3LW, UK
UKHW020448010325
455719UK00015B/478